# Praying the
# Our Father
# Today

# Praying the
# Our Father
# Today

THE PASTORAL PRESS
Washington, DC

ISBN: 0-912405-91-0

© 1991 Ateliers et Presses de Taizé, 71250 Taizé Communauté, France
© 1992 The Pastoral Press

The Pastoral Press
225 Sheridan Street, NW
Washington, DC 20011
(202) 723-1254

The Pastoral Press is the publications division of the National Association
of Pastoral Musicians, a membership organization of musicians and
clergy dedicated to fostering the art of musical liturgy.

Printed in the United States of America

# *Contents*

# "Teach us to pray"

(Lk 11:1)

When the Christian Church was still in its infancy, one of its leaders wrote a letter to some of the newly baptized. In it he encouraged them to keep living lives of love, the touchstone of the new existence they had just entered. He then compared their baptism to a new birth:

> [You have been] reborn not from a perishable seed, but from an imperishable one, through the living and lasting word of God (1 Pt 1:23).

A little further on, continuing with the same image, he gave them some advice for their lives:

> As newborn babies, hunger after unadulterated spiritual milk, so that by it you may grow up into salvation (1 Pt 2:2).

In this letter the Christian life is viewed as a seed of the Gospel planted in us, the source of a new existence which bears fruits of love. For this to happen, however, the seed has to be nourished so that it can grow. The primary question for believers, then, is not "how can I accomplish great feats in

1

my life?" but rather "how can I nourish the seed of the Gospel planted in me so that it will grow and bear fruit?" In other words, what are the *roots* of our faith, the *sources* of the inner life? What enables us to receive new vitality over and over again?

One of the most important of these sources is *prayer*. Prayer is the act by which we place ourselves consciously and voluntarily in the presence of God. It is a time when human beings fully express their identity as believers. When we pray, we implicitly define ourselves as people who do not claim to find our source in ourselves; we come to God with open hands. God is, of course, always with us, and we may wish to live at every moment as if God were the beginning and end of our existence. But forgetfulness is part of the human condition, and our many activities and cares inevitably distract and scatter us. For this reason, those moments when we stop to center ourselves on "the one thing that matters" (see Lk 10:42) are essential.

But how should we pray? We will never stop asking this fundamental question, since prayer is something that we can never claim to have mastered completely; it is not a personal belonging, a reality we have understood once and for all. The world of prayer is a vast universe, and a whole lifetime is scarcely enough to explore a tiny part of it. Methods and advice can be found everywhere, but for the most part they do not satisfy, since they rarely deal with the question on a deep enough level.

The question about prayer is related to another question which is no less essential: who is God? It is obvious that if prayer is by definition a relationship with the One we call God, then it will change according to our view of who God is. Is God a tyrant jealous of my freedom, a schoolteacher obsessed with perfection, or someone who loves me as I am and who wants the best for me? The manner in which we conceive of God is inevitably linked to a particular way of praying.

To these two questions—"Who is God?" and "How should we pray?"—many answers are possible. Each individual can give his or her own answer; in addition, there are the collective answers which have been given by the great world religions in the course of history. If we call ourselves Christians, however, we cannot be content with a purely individual answer. We know that we belong to a faith-community that has existed for centuries, and so we depend not merely upon our own personal intuitions but on the faith of the whole of God's people, a faith that goes back to Abraham, Moses, and the prophets of Israel; we walk in the footsteps of the apostles and disciples of Jesus Christ.

The faith of this community has been passed down from one generation to the next by a living tradition. Inspired writers gave it expression in books which make up what we call the Bible. When we read the Bible and meditate upon it, little by little we begin to glimpse, over centuries of history, the face of God and the features of the human partner that God desires.

Christians also know that everything in the Bible is not on the same level. At the center we find the figure of Jesus Christ, whose life, death, and resurrection reveal God's heart of hearts. It is this figure, whose coming had been prepared from the very beginning and who remains alive in the community that bears his name, who founds the unity of the entire Bible.

It is highly significant, therefore, that one day during his life on earth, Jesus' disciples asked him the very same question that concerns us here:

And it happened that, while he was praying in a certain spot, when he had finished, one of his disciples said to him, "Lord, teach us to pray, just as John taught his disciples" (Lk 11:1).

3

First of all, there is something very simple here that should be pointed out. Jesus prayed. We are used to considering Jesus, the "beloved Son" (Mk 1:11), as someone who lived in a permanent state of spontaneous intimacy with God. It is all the more striking, then, to realize that during his earthly existence, Jesus often took the time to stop and enter into a conscious and explicit relationship with God.

Second, what does the disciple's question actually mean? First he watches Jesus pray, and then he says: "Teach us to pray." Now the disciples were Jews, and therefore for them prayer was an essential part of their lives. They had prayers for all occasions—morning and evening prayers, table blessings, and so on. But here they are asking for something else. They want to learn *Jesus's* prayer. In other words, they wish to be introduced into his own particular relationship with God. They are asking for a prayer that recapitulates the specific message of Jesus and that will clearly identify them as his disciples. So Jesus responds to their request by teaching them the *Our Father* (Lk 11:2-4; Mt 6:9-13).

We can thus understand why, since the beginning of the third century at least (Tertullian), this prayer of Jesus has been considered a recapitulation of the whole Gospel. And yet, when we read it, we cannot can fail to be struck by two things: first, its utter simplicity—it is almost a child's prayer— and second, the fact that practically all of its expressions are characteristic of Jewish prayers with their roots in the Hebrew Scriptures, what Christians call the Old Testament. These two factors may well conceal from us the newness and the power of this prayer.

And yet, from another point of view, here we have something analogous to the mystery of the Incarnation. When Jesus of Nazareth journeyed through the villages of Palestine some two thousand years ago, for many of his contemporaries his uniqueness was not all that obvious. A powerful preacher, healer, or miracle-worker, an impressive rabbi, perhaps even a genius . . . A great man, no doubt, but all in all a human being like us. Only those who took the time to follow him in response to a call that touched the depths of their being were gradually led to discover something of his innermost mystery: "You are the Messiah, the Son of the living God!" (Mt 16:16).

The same can be said of the prayer of Jesus, the Our Father. Only those who take the time to penetrate its mystery will be able to glimpse, beneath the ordinary appearances, beneath the expressions of the day coming from the prayer's biblical and Jewish background, something unique, a kind of gateway into the inner life of God. This is what we are going to attempt in the following pages, by examining the phrases of the Lord's Prayer one after another.

## Questions for Reflection

1. In his preaching Jesus often used the image of a seed. How do the parables of the sower (Mk 4:1-9), the seed that grows by itself (Mk 4:26-29), the weeds and the wheat (Mt 13:24-30), the mustard seed (Mt 13:31-32) help us to understand his message?

2. What conception of God is implicit in Jesus' teaching on prayer in Matthew 6:5-8?

# *Our Father in heaven*

If the Our Father is a recapitulation or summary of the message of Jesus, then the first words are, in their turn, a summary of the whole prayer. They thrust us into the very heart of the Gospel.

First of all, in the Greek text comes the word *Father*. To speak of God— or one of the gods—as a father is something that can be found in a number of civilizations. It is not surprising that, when they attempt to speak of the invisible realm of the divine, human beings borrow images from life here on earth—a father, a mother, a king, a shepherd, and so on. And it is easy to see why God would be referred to as a father: it is a way of describing the divinity as the Source of life.

In ancient Israel too, believers used images taken from daily life to speak of and to God. At the same time, the people of the Bible were deeply aware that their God was someone wholly Other, the Incomparable, a being beyond all the categories of human understanding. Thus the word "father," which implies a relationship of great closeness between God and human beings, is occasionally used in the

Hebrew Scriptures, but always with a certain discretion, and almost never in direct address. Moreover, in the Hebrew Bible, the image of a father does not reflect the fact that God is Creator of the universe, but refers rather to the birth of a people through the event of the Exodus and God's support of this people in all the stages of their existence (Dt 32:6; Is 63:16, 64:7; Mal 2:10). The title is sometimes used to express the special relationship existing between the Lord and the Lord's people; nonetheless, it cannot be said that for Israel this is a customary way of addressing God.

It is all the more striking, then, to look at the Gospels with this as a background. Like every pious Jew, Jesus used the prayers of the Bible, the Psalms (e.g., Mk 15:34). But whenever he prayed in his own words, he began with the word "Father." And, according to Mark 14:36, we know the exact word he used: it was the word *Abba*. At the time of Jesus there were two Semitic languages used in Palestine: Hebrew, the language of the Bible and the liturgy, and Aramaic, the language of everyday life. Now *Abba* is the Aramaic word for father, so we can imagine that the disciples of Jesus were somewhat disconcerted to hear him speak in that way to the living God. It was not customary to call upon the "Holy One of Israel" with such an everyday expression, an expression that could be heard on the lips of children in the streets when they shouted for their "papas." The word must have indeed struck the hearers as something exceptional, for it is among the very few Aramaic expressions that we find in the books of the New Testament. The translation "Father" is simply juxtaposed alongside the Aramaic word, as if the word itself were the bearer of an important message.

What did Jesus wish to express by calling God *Abba* in his prayer? First, the word evokes a unique *intimacy*. Jesus, of course, was not the only Jewish believer to feel that God personally loved and took care of his people. For the Jews, God was never a cold and distant figure. But the relationship between Jesus and the one he called *Abba* was incomparably deeper and more intimate, so that we are justified in speaking of a total communion, a oneness. Later on, when Christians will confess that Jesus is the only Son of God, all they are doing is making explicit what is already contained in the simple word *Abba*.

Second, the use of the word *Abba* is a mark of *trust*, of filial love. Like a little child who turns to its father or mother whenever it encounters the least difficulty, whoever calls God *Abba* sees God as a permanent presence and source of security, especially in times of difficulty. And this confidence is the source of a tremendous freedom: Jesus lives in the certainty that "the Father has placed all things in his hand" (Jn 3:35; see Mt 11:27a).

Two key texts of Saint Paul will now bring us a step further:

When we were immature children, we were slaves to the elements of the world. But when the fullness of time came, God sent his son, born of a woman, born under the Law, to redeem those who were under the Law, to give us the gift of sonship. You are sons: God has sent into our hearts the Spirit of his son that cries out, "*Abba*, Father!" Therefore you are no longer a slave but a son and, if you are a son, then God has made you his heir (Gal 4:3-7).

All who are led by the Spirit of God are sons of God. For you did not receive a spirit of slavery to be ruled once more by fear, but a spirit of sonship, by which we cry out, "*Abba*, Father!" The spirit in person testifies together with our own spirit that we are children of God. But if we are God's children, we are also heirs of God, co-heirs with Christ, if in fact we suffer with him in order to be glorified as well with him (Rom 8:14-17).

In these texts Paul sums up the Christian life as the transition from the condition of a *slave* to that of a *son*. In other words, a relationship with God characterized by fear is transformed into a relationship of trust. And Paul considers this transformation not as the result of something we ourselves have done but as God's own work through Jesus, God's Son. In and through this Son we become in our turn sons (and daughters[*]) of God. By his life, death, and resurrection, Christ brings us into the very same relationship he has with God, "so that he might be the firstborn of many brothers and sisters" (Rom 8:29). He does this, continues Paul, by sending his Spirit into our hearts, the Spirit that cries out in us *"Abba*, Father."

Being able to say *Abba* to God, then, is a way of attesting to the fact that Jesus has brought us into a brand-new relationship with God; it also means expressing this relationship with the word he himself used and then passed on to us. It is a way of confessing our faith in a God who is a Source of trust, who is always there for us, and who wishes for us the fullness of life (Jn 10:10). From the very first word, then, those who pray the Our Father dare, with the trust of faith, to open their hearts to the gift of the Spirit and to occupy the place of Jesus, God's beloved Son.

But whoever dares to enter into Jesus' own prayer in this way, and to call God "Father," must immediately add the word "our." This simple word points as well to a fundamental truth of the Gospel: the new relationship with God has as its immediate consequence a new relationship among hu-

---

[*] It is unfortunate that the word "son" is exclusively masculine, since it is certainly not Paul's intention to limit this new relationship with God to male Christians. In the passage from Romans, Paul uses instead the Greek word *tekna* ("offspring," "children"), a neuter plural; this is also John's usual practice (Jn 1:12, 11:52; 1 Jn 3:1,2,10, 5:2). This has the inconvenience, however, of not emphasizing as strongly the incredible fact that Christ brings us into his very own relationship with God: in and through the *Son*, we become *sons*. In addition, the word "child," though it well expresses the trusting attitude which is the essence of faith (Mk 10:15), has a connotation of immaturity which is, for Paul, the exact opposite of life in Christ, as is clear from Galatians 4:1-3 (see also 1 Cor 13:11, 14:20).

man beings. From now on we are no longer alone; we are members of a community. No individualistic relationship is possible with the God of Jesus Christ. Entering, with Jesus, into a new relationship with God means at the same time discovering that we are linked to all those who are walking on the same road.

One day, in response to a question, Jesus spoke of two great commandments that sum up the whole Torah—love of God and love of neighbor (Mt 22:34-40). If we look closer, however, we discover that in the Gospel these two commandments are seen to be two faces of one and the same reality. "No one who does not love his brother whom he sees can love God, whom he does not see" (1 Jn 4:20b). And the existence of the Christian community, where this mutual love is lived out day after day in concrete fashion, is the existential sign that the God of Jesus Christ is present and active at the heart of human history (see Jn 13:35; 1 Jn 4:12).

Finally, we encounter the expression "in heaven." A typically Jewish way of speaking, these words do not imply that God is far away. They are a way of explaining that, even though we call God "Father," God still remains unique; God is not identical to a human parent. The image we have of God, of course, is formed in part from our experiences with other human beings. A person who has never experienced an authentic human love will have tremendous difficulty in trying to understand God's love for him or her. At the same time, it is essential to realize that God's love goes far beyond any human relationship, all the more so if our human experience of fatherhood has been incomplete or even negative.

In the final analysis, we can understand the words "Our Father" correctly only by looking at Jesus in the Gospels and by discovering his relationship with God. We must allow our understanding of this relationship to complete and, if necessary, to correct our own human experiences of love

11

and fatherhood. Behind the Our Father stands not a human image or analogy, but a living, concrete relationship between Jesus and the One he calls *Abba*. Through Christ this unique relationship becomes accessible to us. When we say yes to Christ, we receive his Spirit and take part in his intimacy with the Father. To put it another way, we enter into the communion, the inner life, of the Holy Trinity. This is why, in the first Christian centuries, the Lord's Prayer was one of the last things taught to those preparing for baptism. They recited it publicly for the first time just after their baptism, during the Easter Vigil, to celebrate the new stage of life they had just entered, a new relationship with God which paralleled their entry into the Christian community.

## Questions for Reflection

1. Even if they do not use the word "father", the Hebrew Scriptures present God as someone who is uttrly trustworthy. How do the following passages explain the reason for this: Psalm 91; Psalm 103; Deuteronomy 7:7-8; Deuteronomy 26:1-11?

2. In what way does the account of Jesus' baptism (Mt 3:13-17) help us understand the first words of the Our Father?

## Hallowed be your name

The first words of the Our Father are followed by a series of petitions. We might think that this represents a kind of backward step with regard to what we have just discovered. If God is our *Abba* who loves us and who is always there to assist us, then why, we might wonder, do we have to ask God for anything? Isn't it unnecessary, or even a sign of doubt?

A teaching of Jesus on prayer can help us here:

And I say to you: Ask, and it will be given to you; seek, and you will find; knock, and the door will be opened for you. For everyone who asks receives, and whoever seeks finds, and the door is opened to anyone who knocks. What father among you, if his son asks him for bread, will give him a stone? Or if he asks for fish, will give him a snake instead of the fish? Or again, if he asks for an egg, will give him a scorpion? If then you, with all your faults, know how to give good gifts to your children, how much more will your Father in heaven give the Holy Spirit to those who ask him (Lk 11:9-13)!

Jesus starts with the analogy of a human father to explain that God is imcomparably greater ("how much more . . ."). Therefore, he says to his disciples, "Ask, and [God*] will give to you." In the Gospel, to ask God for something is not an indication of doubt but just the opposite: a putting into practice, a living out of the confidence and freedom of the children of God. Precisely because God is our *Abba* and we are, in the Son, God's dearly loved sons and daughters, we can and should ask him for whatever we need. This is how we express our trust; this is how the new relationship with God takes shape in the concrete circumstances of our existence. Asking and giving create a reciprocal relationship, with giving more characteristic of God, and asking and receiving more characteristic of human beings. In short, the prayer of petition is a privileged way of collaborating with God.

The petitions of the Our Father can be clearly divided into two parts. The first is characterized by the word "you" (your Name, your Kingdom, your will), and the second by the words "we/us" (give us, forgive us, deliver us). The first three petitions are similar: in fact, they are three slightly different ways of calling for one and the same intervention of God. And, as we shall see, they are not merely human petitions but a participation in the prayer and the mission of the Son, in his "active suffering," in the groaning of the Spirit that arises from the very depths of creation (Rom 8:18-27).

The first petition, "hallowed be your name," is perhaps the most difficult to understand. It is a biblical way of speaking that is quite different from the way we usually express ourselves. What does it mean to ask that God's Name be hallowed or sanctified, in other words, be made or considered holy?

---

*"It will be given you" is an example of the "divine passive." Out of respect, the Jews habitually avoided pronouncing the divine Name. It would have been obvious to them, however, that God is in fact the subject of this phrase.

We can begin by exploring the meaning of *names* in the Bible. A name is never just a simple word or label, as is often the case for us. In the Bible, a name is part of the reality of a person or thing; it reveals its secret; it manifests its being, its *identity*. This is why, when someone encounters God, they sometimes receive a new name. Their life has been changed, and they have thus acquired a new identity.

Similarly, and to an even greater degree, God's Name is not just a word. The divine Name is God viewed from a certain angle; it is the face of God turned toward his people. Thus we read in the writings of the Deuteronomic school that God's Name dwells in the Temple of Jerusalem (Dt 12:11, 14:23; 1 Kg 3:2, 5:17). This does not mean, to be sure, that a mere word is sitting in this site. It expresses rather the believer's conviction that the Temple is the place where God is manifested in a special way, where God communicates with his people.

God's presence in Israel is not limited to the realm of worship, however, as the following key text explains:

> The Lord will establish you as his holy people, as he promised you on oath, if you keep the commands of the Lord your God and walk in his ways. Then all the peoples on earth will see that *you are called by the Name of the Lord*, and they will fear you (Dt 28:9-10).

God creates a people, a people called by God's Name. In other words, God's identity is revealed to "all the peoples on earth" through the existence of one people chosen for that purpose. At the same time, to be called by God's Name is not something automatic. The people have to "keep the commands of the Lord . . . and walk in his ways," so that they will communicate to the rest of the world a correct image of God.

What happens, we may ask, if God's people do not live according to the will of the Lord? In that case, they become a kind of living contradiction, no longer faithfully mirroring the Source of their existence as a people; they no longer make it possible for others to know God as God really is. In biblical terms, they *profane the Name of the Lord* (Lv 23:31ff.; Is 52:5). A gap arises between the reality of the living God and the image of God transmitted by his people through the lives they lead.

Several centuries before Christ, the prophet Ezekiel had to deal with just such a situation. His words provide, in fact, the best commentary on this first petition of the Lord's Prayer. The prophet is undertaking his mission during the exile in Babylon. It is a very difficult time in the life of Israel when it no longer exists as an independent nation. The prophet explains the reasons for this state of affairs:

> The word of the Lord came to me: Son of man, when the people of Israel were living in their own land, they defiled it by their conduct and their actions ... So I dispersed them among the nations, and they were scattered among the countries ... And wherever they went among the nations they profaned my holy Name, for it was said of them, "These are the Lord's people, and yet they had to leave his land" (Ez 36:16-20).

On account of your infidelity and the political disaster that followed, says the Lord by the mouth of the prophet, you have profaned my holy Name. But, God continues, I cannot allow things to go on like that; I must do something:

> I had concern for my holy Name, which the house of Israel profaned among the nations where they had gone. Therefore say to the house of Israel: This is what the Sovereign Lord says: It is not for your sake, O house of Israel, that I am going to do these things, but for the sake of my holy Name, which you have profaned among the nations where you have gone (36:21-22).

In other words, the people have no right to ask God to take care of them. The people deserve nothing, but God will do it anyway to be faithful to his own identity. God is the God of mercy and justice, and has to act accordingly. And so the prophet continues:

> I will show the holiness of ("hallow") my great name, which has been profaned among the nations, the Name you have profaned among them. Then the nations will know that I am the Lord, declares the Sovereign Lord, when I show myself holy through you before their eyes. For I will take you out of the nations; I will gather you from all the countries and bring you back into your own land. I will sprinkle clean water on you, and you will be clean; I will cleanse you from all your impurities and from all your idols (36:23-25).

God will take steps to save his people. God will bring the exiles back home and give them a new beginning by forgiving their sins. In this way, God's identity will become clear to the world. And yet, the prophet is aware that this will not solve the problem once and for all. What will keep the nation from forgetting the Lord in the future, as it did in the past? So Ezekiel looks forward to a time when God will transform the people from within, changing their hearts and placing God's own breath of life, his Spirit, within their being. Then the people will truly be able to hallow God's Name; they will live in such a way that the identity of their God becomes clearly visible:

> I will give you a new heart and put a new spirit in you; I will remove from you your heart of stone and give you a heart of flesh. And I will put my Spirit in you and move you to follow my decrees and be careful to keep my laws. You will live in the land I gave your forefathers; you will be my people, and I will be your God (36:26-28).

It is not hard to see why the first Christians saw the fulfillment of this prophecy in the Gospel of Jesus Christ. First, Jesus is "the One who comes in the Name of the Lord" (Mk 11:9). In other words, he reveals to human beings the true identity of God; he communicates to us God's real Name. We may think here of the word *Abba*, of course, but in fact the true Name of God revealed by Jesus is not some title or word spoken by lips; it is the whole of his life. Jesus' entire existence, which is summed up in his death and resurrection, insofar as this shows us in what absolute love consists (Jn 13:1), provides the answer to the question "who is God?" The mission of Jesus is one of "manifesting the Name of God" (Jn 17:6), in "making known the Name" (Jn 17:26).

In John's Gospel (12:23-32) there comes a time when some people of other nations want to see Jesus. The Jewish people believed that the day would come when the nations would go up to Jerusalem, to worship the God of Israel and to accept God's teachings. This was considered a sign that the end of the age was at hand (Is 2:2-4, 60; Zec 8:20-23, 14:16-19). From the simple fact that non-Jews are interested in him, Jesus realizes that the hour of his glorification has come, in other words, the full manifestation of his identity. For this reason, he speaks of his imminent death and resurrection, using the image of the seed that has fallen to the ground and died so as to bear much fruit. Immediately afterwards, he cries out, "Father, glorify your Name!" The meaning of this expression is very close to "hallow" (make holy) your Name." Jesus' death and resurrection, by revealing his true identity as the Son, will at the same time fully reveal the identity of God.

We have seen that, in the Hebrew Scriptures, Israel is called by God's Name either to profane or to hallow it. The same is true for us as disciples of Christ. At the end of his life, Jesus prays to the Father for his disciples who are still in the world: "Keep them in your Name that you gave to me, so that they may be one as we [are one]" (Jn 17:11b). And the most important sign that we bear this Name, that we belong to God, is the communion that exists between us, a communion rooted in the very being of God ("one as we are one"). By remaining in that communion through the practice of mutual love, Christians are a flesh-and-blood icon for the world of the living God; they make God's Name present in an authentic way (see Jn 13:34-35, 17:20-23).

To sum up, when we pray "hallowed be your Name," we are asking God to let all humanity discover his true identity and recognize God as their *Abba*. We pray that all may see God as a Source of trust and love. Through this prayer we express the desire that the new relationship with God into which we have entered by the coming of Christ and the gift of the Spirit may be broadened to include all creation. At the same time, we understand that this sanctification of God's Name takes place through our existence. We ask God to make use of our lives to communicate his true identity. We ask God to enable us to be beings who are truly in the divine image, who faithfully transmit something of who God is.

## Questions for Reflection

1. At two key moments of his life, Moses receives a revelation of God's Name (Ex 3:14, 34:6). What is the significance of these "names" he receives?

2. The first Christians were sometimes known as "those who call upon the Name of the Lord" (Acts 9:14,21; 22:16; 1 Cor 1:2; 2 Tim 2:22). What light does the prophecy of Joel (Jl 2:28-32; see Acts 2:17-21) and the hymn in Philippians (Phil 2:6-11) shed upon this title?

3. How can we make our lives more transparent to the light of God?

# Your Kingdom come

The second petition of the Lord's Prayer, "may your Kingdom come," refers basically to the same reality as the preceding one, but views it from a different angle. For it is not enough to know the true identity of God; this knowledge must lead us to live in a certain way. Here then, we shift from a religious image, making holy God's Name, to a political one, the Kingdom or Reign of God. Two juxtaposed oracles of the prophet called Second Isaiah will allow us to understand the unity between these two languages.

"And now what do I have here?" declares the Lord. "For my people have been taken away for nothing, and those who rule them mock," declares the Lord. "And all day long my Name is constantly blasphemed. Therefore my people will know my Name; therefore in that day they will know that it is I who foretold it. Yes, it is I."

How beautiful on the mountains are the feet of those who bring good news, who proclaim peace, who bring good tidings, who proclaim salvation, who say to Zion, "Your God reigns!" (Is 52:5-7).

First, along the lines of Ezekiel 36, God explains that the divine Name has been profaned by the disastrous situation of the people exiled in Babylon. Nonetheless, soon God is going to set things right: "my people will know my Name." This is an announcement of imminent salvation, and the following verse expands upon this in a different language: it will be a time of peace, of happiness, summed up in the cry: "Your God reigns!" On that day, the world as it is in reality will be identical with the world as God wishes it to be.

In subsequent Jewish tradition, the future time of salvation is often called the Reign (or Kingdom, or Rule) of God. The gospel writers, in turn, were inspired by Isaiah 52:7 when they spoke of the coming of Jesus Christ and his "good news" of the imminent arrival of the Reign of God (Mk 1:14-15).

Another text from the book of Isaiah describes this Reign:

> In the last days
> the mountain of the Lord's temple will be established
> as chief among the mountains;
> it will be raised above the hills,
> and all nations will stream to it.
> Many peoples will come and say,
> "Come, let us go up to the mountain of the Lord,
> to the house of the God of Jacob.
> He will teach us his ways,
> so that we may walk in his paths."
> The law will go out from Zion,
> the word of the Lord from Jerusalem.
> He will judge between the nations
> and will settle disputes for many peoples.
> They will beat their swords into plowshares
> and their spears into pruning hooks.
> Nation will not take up sword against nation,
> nor will they train for war anymore.
> (Is 2:2-4 = Mi 4:1-3)

The prophet communicates his vision of a future when all nations will go up to Jerusalem to be taught by God, to learn to walk in God's paths. Although the words "king" or "reign" are not found in this passage, God is said to "judge" and to "settle disputes," two royal functions par excellence. There will follow an era of peace and justice for the whole world, a consequence of the fact that all will accept God as their guide and arbitrator. The Reign of Kingdom of God is thus shown to be a *new world order* open to all, an order that follows from knowledge of God and God's ways.

How can this beautiful vision become a reality? Among the Jewish people, different answers were given to this question. For some, the establishment of the Kingdom could only be the work of God alone. Perhaps it would even entail a complete transformation of the universe as we know it. All that human beings could do was to live their lives in an attitude of ardent expectation and pray for its coming. At the other extreme, some saw the coming of the Kingdom as the consequence of a political revolution; by taking up arms and expelling the enemies of Israel from the Promised Land, the people would force God's hand, so to speak, obliging him to act in their favor. Between these two extremes, there was undoubtedly a whole gamut of different opinions.

At the time of Jesus, an influential group among the Jewish people was longing for God's Kingdom with all its heart. This group felt that the way to hasten the coming of this Kingdom was to begin already, here and now, to anticipate it in the concrete circumstances of one's daily life. This could be done by observing the commandments, by living as far as possible according to the Torah, the Law of the Lord. These people chose, as they put it, "to take upon themselves the yoke of the Torah." Those who spoke this way were known as the Pharisees; in a certain sense, they were not too far from Jesus' own view of things.

For Jesus used the image of the Kingdom of God to express the heart of his message. At the same time, he transformed the image to make it conform to the newness of his vision. It is not the purpose of this book to examine all the dimensions of Jesus' understanding of the Kingdom of God. Such an undertaking is all the more difficult since Jesus never provided a definition but spoke about the Kingdom for the most part by means of stories and images, the parables. Let us try, however, to give a few important indications of the way Jesus saw the Kingdom of God.

First of all, for Jesus the Kingdom of God will not arrive by means of human violence or power. It has nothing in common with a nationalistic outlook, a victory for some and a defeat for others. As Jesus explained to the Roman governor, it is not a kingdom according to the criteria of this world (Jn 18:36).

Second, for Jesus the Kingdom of God always retains its universalistic outlook. It is like a tree which offers shelter to all the birds in the sky (Lk 13:19), a net that gathers in "all kinds of things" (Mt 13:47), a banquet to which even paupers and the handicapped are invited (Lk 14:13,21). In short, it is a reality open to all.

Finally, a third characteristic of the Kingdom announced by Jesus is perhaps the most original of all. For him, the Kingdom is certainly an object of deep longing, a future reality which the Father will bring about in the his own time and by means known to him alone (e.g., Mt 25:13; Lk 21:31). But at the same time, it is a reality already "at hand" (Mk 1:15); in some sense it has already begun with his coming. To express this seeming paradox, Jesus uses images like the tiny seed that becomes a large tree and the yeast that raises a huge mass of dough (Mt 13:31-33).

Jesus speaks of God's Reign as something already at work in the world, but in a hidden, mysterious manner; though it cannot be distinguished by outward signs (Lk 17:20-21), it nonetheless requires a radical commitment, a conversion of the heart. Those who have eyes to see and ears to hear the mystery of the Kingdom present in Jesus become, in their turn, subjects of that Kingdom. By their yes to Jesus, they prepare the way for the Kingdom and allow it to emerge from hiddenness into the light of day. This explains the urgency of Jesus' call, for with his coming the hour of God has already struck.

## Questions for Reflection

1.  What would be the features of a world that is following the guidance of God?

2.  Sometimes the prophecies describing Israel's future hope speak of an ideal king, the "Messiah" or Anointed One, who would come to help usher in the new age. How do the following texts help us to understand the characteristics of the Kingdom of God and the mission of Jesus Christ: Isaiah 11:1-9; Psalm 72; Zechariah 9:9-10?

3.  Jesus explained to Nicodemus that it was not possible to enter the Kingdom of God without a new birth, a birth from above (Jn 3). Why?

## Your will
## be done . . .

In the oracle of Isaiah 2:2-4 quoted above, the dawning of a world of peace and reconciliation comes about when "all nations" set out to find and walk in "God's paths." The text thus helps us to see the close link between the third petition of the Lord's Prayer (absent, incidentally, from Luke's version) and the preceding phrase. To put it in a nutshell: the Kingdom of God, the new world order, becomes a reality when people live according to the will of God.

The Hebrew Scriptures speak of God's will with two different nuances, one more active and the other more passive. First, we find the expression "to do the will of God" (e.g., Ps 40:8; 119:112; 143:10). In Hebrew this means litterally "to do what is pleasing to God, to accomplish God's good pleasure." This reminds us that it is not a question of obeying an abstract law but rather of living out the consequences of a personal relationship. If we love someone, we spontaneously try to do whatever pleases that person, to act in a way that makes that person happy.

But we can also invert the image. If God loves us, then what makes God happy is for us to attain the fullness of life, to find happiness, not in a superficial way but by becoming who we are truly meant to be. And this brings us to the second meaning of the expression "the will of God." It can refer to God's overarching intention or plan for the universe and for the whole human race, as well as for each and every one of us (see Eph 1:9-10).

To speak of God's designs or plan is a way of expressing the fact that God has created us for a reason, that our life has a meaning: the existence of the universe and of every creature has a purpose willed by the goodness of God. What happens to us and what we do is not a matter of indifference to God. God has created us to live in communion with him. But the image would lead us astray if we saw it as some sort of book where everything was written down ahead of time, a reality already prepared in advance for us and requiring us merely to follow blindly the way that has been traced out. Once again, a human comparison may help. Parents who truly love their children undoubtedly have certain hopes and expectations for them. They want their children to develop their abilities fully; what their children do matters to them. At the same time, loving parents do not force their children to act in a certain way; they wish their children to use their gifts fully to become mature and responsible adults.

The same is true of God, and to an even greater degree. God desires our happiness. But, unlike human parents, it is God who is responsible for our gifts, and one of the greatest of these is freedom. To fulfill God's plan, therefore, we have to become fully ourselves by developing our gifts. God's plan does not shackle our freedom; it is a call for us to use our freedom to become beings who are more and more in God's image, capable of loving and serving. God's will can never be separated from God's love; it is the manner in which this love takes concrete form by stages in our own lives and in the history of the world.

The fact that God's will does not crush our human wills, but rather liberates them, can seem paradoxical if we remain on a purely theoretical level. The example of Jesus, above all in John's Gospel, helps us understand that in practice no contradiction in fact exists. On the one hand, Jesus states that he does not seek his own will but only his Father's; he does nothing by himself (Jn 5:19,30, 8:28,42b, 12:49). On the other hand, Jesus is the freest person imaginable: the Father always listens to him (Jn 11:42) and has placed all things in his hands (Jn 13:3, 5:20-22,26-27).

This mystery of the Son's freedom expressing itself in obedience to the Father's will appears as well in the following words of Jesus: "My food is to do the will of the One who sent me and to bring his work to completion" (Jn 4:34). Far from being something that oppresses him or limits his freedom, the discovery and the practice of God's will is for Jesus a source of life and energy, a "food." The Father's will is, for him, the love of God translated into the concrete circumstances of his existence as a call to action, an impulse to go forward.

This is true even at the most difficult hour of Jesus' life, in Gethsemane (Mk 14:32-42). There he experiences the full extent and power of evil. Nonetheless he prays, "*Abba* ... not what I want, but what you want!" It is essential to understand that there is nothing fatalistic about this prayer: it is not a half-hearted consent to "the lesser of two evils" or because there is no alternative. Jesus' response here is an act of trust made in the depths of the night. His life is rooted in the conviction that God is his *Abba* who wants what is best for him and for the world, in spite of contradictory appearances. The prayer of Gethsemane is Jesus' attempt to discern, behind these appearances, the victory of love as a road for him to follow. And trust in God is the only attitude that makes this discernment possible.

How can we, in our turn, do the will of God? An inexhaustible question, that cannot be reduced to a rule or a method. A well-known passage of Matthew's Gospel can point us in the right direction:

> You are the light of the world. A city set on a hill cannot be hidden. And no one lights a lamp and puts it under a basket, but rather on the lampstand, and it gives light to all in the house. In the same way, let your light shine out, so that people will see your good works and give glory to your Father in heaven (Mt 5:14-16).

Jesus compares his disciples to light. Then, to the question "What should we do?" the reply is not without humor: "You must shine!" Light can scarcely do anything else, even without trying very hard! And with the second image, that of the city on a hill, Jesus in fact assures us that it is far more difficult, even impossible, to prevent this radiance from being seen once it exists. Here, as so often in the Gospels, Jesus replies to our questions by transforming them. The real question is seen to be on another level. It is not a matter of dreaming up innumerable projects but of discovering how to be light.

Fortunately, Jesus gives us the answer to this other question when he tells us, "I am the light of the world" (Jn 8:12). To the extent that we live united with him, we receive from him that light which will gradually transform us into his image (2 Cor 3:18). Then we will bear fruit, the "good works" which will "give glory to God," in other words, will make him known to others as he truly is. Acting has its importance, but it does not possess its center in itself. It follows directly from our identity as children of God like light radiating from a lamp. Doing the will of God means above all letting God do his will in and through us (see Jn 6:28-29; Phil 2:13; Heb 13:21).

## Questions for Reflection

1. Based on the following texts, what characterizes those who do the will of God: Psalm 15; Psalm 131; Genesis 12:1-4 and Hebrews 11:8-10 (Abraham); Luke 1:26-38 (Mary); Luke 10:29-37?

2. Saint Paul writes, "God's will is that you be holy" (1 Thes 4:3). How do these words help us better to understand the unity of the first part of the Our Father?

## . . . on earth
## as in heaven

Before examining the second part of the Lord's Prayer, let us stop for a moment to sum up our discoveries. We have seen that the first words of the prayer place us at the very heart of the Gospel: through Christ and by the gift of his Spirit, we enter into a brand-new relationship with God ("Father") that is immediately translated into a new relationship among human beings ("our").

But this new relationship, made up of trust and love, is not a privilege reserved to a chosen few. For this reason, the phrases that follow the words "Our Father in heaven" ask for the relationship to be widened to embrace all humanity, to include the whole of creation. We ask God to reveal his true identity (his Name) to all, so that the whole human race can live according to his loving will and thus allow a new world order to come about (God's Kingdom).

In a certain sense, the last words of this part of the prayer sum up its meaning very well: "on earth as in heaven." Heaven stands for God, and in these three petitions we pray for the reality of God to penetrate the earth more and more; we ask that God's love may transform an indifferent or hostile world into a Kingdom of justice and peace. This communion between heaven and earth, prepared in the course of centuries, entered a decisive phase with the coming of the Son of God as one of us (Lk 2:14).It continues in the existence of the community of believers, the church, a priestly people (1 Pt 2:5,9; Ex19:6) which shares the mission of Christ to bring the Good News of God's love to the "very ends of the earth" (Acts 1:8).

We have also seen that this prayer is likewise a *commitment*. It is as if we said to God: "Take my life so that, through me, something of your love, of your light, can be communicated to others. Enable me to reveal your Life in the simple events of my own existence."

A question can then arise. Aware as we are of our fragility, conscious of our limits, how can we dare make such a commitment?Where will we find the strength to keep it? The answer to this important question is given in the second part of the prayer. There we shift from "you" to "us." But for all that, it is not a self-centered prayer; we are not asking for things to satisfy our personal pleasure. One the contrary, in the second part of the Our Father, we ask for all we need to live out the commitment that we have made in the first part.

To understand the Lord's Prayer correctly, it is essential to realize its unity. It is not merely the case, as is so often said, that the first part is devoted to God and the second part to human needs. After the Incarnation, God and human beings can no longer be separated in this way. The Our Father is one prayer, not two; after making our own the prayer of the Son, we ask for the gifts that will allow us to participate in Christ's mission, to set out on the road with him. To put it another way, we are the Body of Christ; he is our Head (see Col 1:18). In the first part of the Our Father, we united ourselves to the prayer of the Head; the second part is the prayer of the Body.

## Question for Reflection

1. How did Christ himself live the first part of the Our Father during his life on earth?

*Give us this day
our daily bread
(tomorrow's bread)*

The first of the great gifts we ask of God is the gift of *bread*. It should first be pointed out that the word "bread" in Hebrew refers to all that is necessary for life—food, clothing, shelter... And the Bible assures us that, even though human beings must work to earn their bread "by the sweat of their brow" (Gn 3:17-19), it comes in the final analysis from God, "who gives bread to every creature, for eternal is his love" (Ps 136:25; see Ps 22:26; 104:27f.; 107:9; 111:5; 145:15f.).

Understanding this phrase of the Lord's Prayer is made more complicated by the fact that it includes a word whose exact meaning we do not know. This is the Greek word *epiousios*, which is found only here in the entire New Testament. There are two principal interpretations of the word. The first is more common: *daily* bread, the bread we need *today*. But we can also find reasons to translate the phrase: *tomorrow's* bread, bread for the future. In this case, what would the petition mean? Did not Jesus tell us "don't worry about tomorrow" (Mt 6:34)? For this reason, those who favor the second interpretation usually give it a spiritual explanation. "Tomorrow's bread" is the bread of the world to come, the bread of God's Kingdom, the bread of the Promised Land. In this case, the petition would simply be another way of praying for the coming of the Kingdom. Can we decide between the two possibilities?

I believe that both interpretations are correct in part, and that both point to a deeper truth. I say this not merely from a spirit of compromise, but from a reflection on the meaning of bread in the Bible. Let us undertake this reflection together, starting from three well-known passages: the story of manna in the wilderness (Ex 16); the temptation of Jesus regarding bread (Mt 4:2-4); and finally the story of the multiplication of the loaves, followed by a discourse on the bread of life (Jn 6).

We begin with the Exodus story. On the road to the Promised Land, the Israelites find themselves in a difficult situation. They are starving. This causes them to criticize Moses and Aaron, but indirectly it is God they are attacking. At that moment, in the wilderness, a miraculous event occurs. Food falls on the ground during the night, a mysterious "bread" the people call "manna," which means literally "what is it?"

First of all, this bread is a material reality, something to feed the starving people and allow them to continue their journey. At the same time, it is something more. It comes from *heaven*, in other words, directly from God (Ex 16:4). Furthermore, we are told that it tasted like *honey* (Ex 16:31). When we find honey in the Bible, we are automatically led to think about the Promised Land, "the land of milk and honey." The manna is thus a kind of foretaste of the Promised Land; it is "tomorrow's bread" which suddenly appears in the people's life today, to give them strength and courage for their pilgrimage.

Two other details are significant here. First, the manna makes possible a miraculous experience of sharing, of perfect solidarity. We read that "those who gathered much did not have too much, and those who gathered little did not have too little; each gathered as much as they needed" (Ex

16:18). In this isolated place, far from civilization, there is a kind of anticipation of the Kingdom of God, a world of justice become reality. In addition, the manna cannot be accumulated or stored up for a rainy day. Some people try to keep it for the following day, and it becomes rotten and full of worms (Ex 16:20).

Let us now turn to the story of Jesus in the wilderness (Mt 4:2-4). He too is hungry, and the Tempter tries to create a division between Jesus and his Father by whispering in Jesus' ear the suggestion that he solve the problem by himself. Instead of living in trust, would it not be more efficient to deal with matters by spectacular feats of power? For his part, Jesus responds with some simple words from Scripture: "Man does not live on bread alone but on every word that comes from the mouth of God."

If we replace this quotation in its context, chapter 8 of the Book of Deuteronomy, we discover a discourse on the lessons the people of Israel were to learn by their pilgrimage in the desert. And the verse in question (Dt 8:3) refers precisely to the story of the manna. The text quoted by Jesus, therefore, contrary to what we might imagine at first glance, does not make a distinction between material bread (presumably less important) and spiritual food (a gift from God). Jesus is not claiming that people can get along without bread; he is affirming that trust in God is what really matters, since God is the true source of *all* that we need, both spiritual and material realities. This verse of Deuteronomy is an invitation to discern, behind the things of this world, the presence and the activity of God that give them consistency; it is a call to discover in this world the Kingdom of God already present.

Finally, let us look at the sixth chapter of John's Gospel. A large crowd follows Jesus to a lonely place, to a "mountain" on the other side of the lake, far from the town. Jesus feeds them miraculously with five loaves of bread. Once again, we are dealing with material bread, but allusions to Sinai (the mountain, Jn 6:3), and the coming of Passover (Jn 6:4) point to another order of reality.

This becomes explicit in the following discourse. Jesus says to the crowds, "Work not for perishable food, but for food that lasts to eternal life, which the Son of Man will give you" (Jn 6:27). Then he explains that he is the true manna, the bread from God that gives life to the world. And, at the end, his words become even more concrete, shockingly so: "Unless you eat the flesh of the Son of Man and drink his blood, you will not have life in you" (Jn 6:53). Only in the light of the resurrection will the disciples fully understand the meaning of these words. Then they will realize that Jesus was talking about his life given on the cross and communicated to us, in the sacrament of the eucharist, by communion in this body handed over to death for us and this blood shed for us.

In all three texts, bread is seen as something material, to be sure, but something pointing beyond itself to another order of things, to God as the Source of our life. The Bible does not separate the "material" and the "spiritual" to downplay or despise the former and to exalt the latter. The biblical vision is different: it takes seriously the things of this world, while at the same time looking behind them to the presence of God which gives them existence and meaning. It emphasizes communion with God, trust in God, as the fundamental reality which sustains us on our journey.

It is likewise interesting to note that, in these passages, the gift of bread always occurs in an uninhabited place. In the desert, human beings are able to welcome things as gifts from God. When things are too comfortable and easy, however, we are more likely than not to pass by what is essential. This is the logic of the Beatitudes: "Happy are you who are hungry (for justice): you will be filled" (Lk 6:21; Mt 5:6). Being hungry is not good in itself, far from it; but, through Christ, this place of deprivation, this place where our need manifests itself, becomes the point at which God enters the world.

To sum up, when we pray "give us this day our daily (tomorrow's) bread," we are asking God to sustain us during our pilgrimage with Christ, so that we may be able to bring God's living water, God's light, God's love, into the deserts of this world. This support does not exclude material bread, of course, but at the same time it aims further. What is the food that will help us to live as God's witnesses in the world? It is the word of God that we find in the Bible; it is prayer; it is mutual love between Christians, the support of others; and it is the eucharist that recapitulates all these other kinds of "bread." In short, it is Christ Jesus himself, the "living bread" who nourishes and sustains us by giving us, here on earth, a foretaste of heaven.

By this petition of the Lord's Prayer, we also commit ourselves to live fully in the present and to find God in each new day. Luke's version ("give us each day") emphasizes the aspect of journey, of setting out day after day, whereas Matthew's underlines the urgency of the present day, but both invite us to live lives of trust in God, and not to get caught up in what is not essential.

## Questions for Reflection

1. Read 1 Kings 19:1-8. What "desert experiences" have I had? In other words, at what times or places did I feel more strongly the need for God?

2. In these situations, how did God nourish me? What bread does God offer me for my own faith journey?

43

*And forgive us
our debts
as we also have
forgiven
our debtors*

Anyone who tries to live fully in God's present day will inevitably have to deal with his or her own past. All of us have a past history made up, among other things, of mistakes, regrets, wounds inflicted or received—in short, we carry around with us a load of excess baggage which weighs us down and holds us back. For this reason, the second great gift for which we ask God in the Our Father, after that of bread, is the gift of *forgiveness*. In other words, we open our hearts to God's healing and re-creating love which enables us to start all over again by removing from our shoulders the burden of the past.

In the Bible, there are several different ways to speak about human wrongdoing. Here, as on other occasions, Jesus uses the image of a *debt*. Why this image? A clue is given in the parable of the talents (Mt 25:14ff.). Before leaving on a journey, a rich man entrusts a large sum of money to three of his servants, to each according to his abilities. Two of them use the money to earn more. The third, paralyzed by fear, digs a hole and buries his money so as not to lose it. Upon his return, the master praises the first two servants and blames the third. In other words, for Jesus, what is regrettable is human beings who do not develop the gifts given them by God, who have no confidence in themselves because they have no confidence in their God. Created in the image of God and called to transmit to others what we have received, we can hide this radiance out of egotism or out of fear.

Another parable, that of the unforgiving servant (Mt 18:23ff.) is an excellent commentary on this petition of the Lord's Prayer. The story tells of a king who cancels his servant's debt, and then the servant refuses to forgive in his turn a fellow-servant who owes him money. Here I want to bring out just one detail. We read that the servant owed his master ten thousand talents. Today, such a sum would amount to more than sixty million dollars. There was probably not that much money in all of Palestine in those days. So why this exaggeration? On the one hand, it is to emphasize the difference between what the king forgave his servant and what the servant had to forgive, a hundred denarii, about two hundred dollars. There is no common measure between what God gives to us and what we are asked to give in turn. Second, it is also a way of saying that we will never be able to settle accounts with God, "I've done enough now; don't expect anything else." We will always have to turn to God to receive his unlimited forgiveness; in the final analysis, this is our only hope.

The fact that God forgives, that the Lord is a merciful God, is not something unique to the New Testament. From the beginning, Israel knew that its God was kind and compassionate. Israel's entire history points it in this direction. We saw this in the prophecy in Ezekiel 36: after each false step, God enters once again into human history to put things right, to set his people back on course. The word "mercy" is even a component of God's Name (Ex 34:6; Ps 86:15; Ps 103:8; see also Dt 4:31; Ps 51:1; Ps 78:38). It is true that Jesus, by giving his life to the very end, shows us just how far God's forgiveness goes; the cross reveals a mercy that has no limits because it consents to give everything (Jn 15:13). Nevertheless, God's mercy has a long history in Israel, as well as in Islam.

In what, then, does the uniqueness of the Gospel consist? We find the answer in a verse from Saint Luke: "Be merciful, just as your Father is merciful" (Lk 6:36; see Mt 5:7). What is really new is not that God is merciful, but that we can be merciful like God, that we can be truly in God's image.

After two thousand years of Christianity, we have heard the words love and forgiveness so often that we may even consider them the most normal things in the world. We may think this, even if in fact we do not put them into practice. Jesus does not share this view of things, however. He tells us that the "normal" way people act is to love those who love them, to treat well those who treat them well (Mt 5:43-47). The eternal human tendency is to divide people into two categories—my friends and my enemies (or those I do not care about)—and to behave towards them in consequence. Where there is something else, where there is the capacity to love those who hate us, to forgive those who keep on hurting us, then something more than the merely human is present. In such a situation God is actively at work.

The Our Father also speaks about the link between God's forgiveness and our forgiveness of others. But it is very important to understand in just what this link consists. A superficial reading could give us the idea that God's forgiveness comes in the second place as a response to our forgiveness, a kind of reward for good behavior. "Forgive me, Lord, since I myself am kind and compassionate." Now if this were the case, the Lord's Prayer would be in flagrant contradiction with the overall message of the New Testament. It would offer as a model for Christian behavior not the tax-collector, but the Pharisee of the well-known parable of Saint Luke (Lk 18:9-14). For Jesus, God's love is always first; a selfless love practiced by humans, essential though it is, can only be a consequence of hearts opened to God's love, to God's Spirit. The fourth chapter of John's First Letter is quite clear in this regard:

> My dear friends, let us love one another, since love comes from God, and whoever loves is born of God and knows God ... Love consists in this: not that we loved God, but that he loved us and sent his Son for the forgiveness of our sins ... Let us love, since he loved us first. If someone says, "I love God," and hates his brother, he is a liar. For a person who does not love his brother, whom he has seen, cannot love God, whom he has not seen. And we have this commandment from him: whoever loves God must also love his brother (1 Jn 4:7, 10, 19-21).

"God loved us first," and sent the Son to bring us into the embrace of divine love when we were "sinners," namely, beings incapable of loving (Rom 5:8). But John does not stop there; he goes on to say that we are called in turn to love (1 Jn 4:11). The love and forgiveness that we show to our brothers and sisters is the sign of the authenticity of our love for God; it is also the touchstone of our understanding of God's great love for us. "Whoever loves ... knows God" (1 Jn 4:7; see 1 Jn 4:12).

Here we enter into the mystery of the "new commandment" of mutual love (Jn 13:34-35). This commandment is not new because it had never been expressed before: does not the Torah state unequivocally "You shall love your neighbor as yourself" (Lv 19:18)? The newness is expressed in the words "love ... as I have loved you." The commandment is new because it is not merely an *order* imposed from without; it is at the same time, and even more, an inner *gift*. Jesus gives us his love, his Spirit that comes from the Father and that will transform us little by little into beings able to love and to forgive in the image of God. Our love for others is the proof that we are in communion with Christ (Jn 13:35), who makes the Father's love present in our world (Jn 17:23).

In this petition of the Our Father, there is a confirmation of what has just been said. Four times, in a very short sentence, we encounter the words "we," "us," or "our." In our discussion of the first words of the Lord's Prayer, we investigated the meaning of the word "our": the new relationship with God into which Jesus brings us involves a new relationship among human beings. Henceforth we are members of a community; we are the church. It is therefore not as isolated individuals but as the church that we ask God for forgiveness. The church, however, is in no way a human elite; it is made up of men and women who have already "recognized and believed in the love God has for them" (see 1 Jn 4:16) and who try to put this love into practice in their daily lives.

Why, then, must we pray for God's forgiveness if, as members of the church, we have already encountered and accepted it? The answer is given once again in the story of the manna in the wilderness. Spiritual gifts cannot be received once and for all, and then stored up for a future date. Love can never become my private possession: the only way to receive it is to give it. To the extent that we share generously with others the forgiveness God has shown to us, we are able to keep on asking God to shower upon us this forgiveness (see Lk 6:38). We are not only *able* to do this, we *need* to do so in order to love still more. To receive my love, God says to us in effect, you have to keep on loving; you have to put into practice the little you have already understood of my Gospel. One step forward will lead the way to other steps. The important thing is to begin, even with very little, almost nothing. Perhaps this is what those enigmatic words of Christ mean: "To everyone who has, more and more will be given; but to those who do not have, even what they have will be taken away from them" (Mt 25:29; Lk 19:26).

A final remark: to forgive those who have hurt us, to forgive them truly and not just with our lips, we often need to accomplish a long inner journey. During this time, when we feel we are not yet able to forgive, can we still pray the

49

Lord's Prayer? Yes, because even the beginning of a desire to wish to forgive is already a consequence of God's grace in us. Moreover, we must not forget that the Our Father is not an individualistic prayer but the prayer of the community of the church. In an ancient Christian prayer we find these words: "Look not on my sins but on the faith of your church." We are sustained by the trust and the forgiveness of the whole church. To emphasize clearly the permanent presence of God's forgiveness in our midst, the church has set apart ministers to proclaim this forgiveness in a very personal way in the sacrament of reconciliation. This sacrament exists to make it clear to us that God's forgiveness is always available for the asking, even when subjectively we hardly dare believe it. It is like a promise for the future already at our disposition now, to allow us to be fully present in God's today.

## Questions for Reflection

1. According to the following texts, what are the consequences of God's forgiveness in our life: Mark 2:1-17; Luke 7:36-50?

2. Where do we see around us human beings divided into two camps, "friends" and "enemies"? How can we accomplish signs of reconciliation, in the image of a God "who is kind even to the ungrateful" (Lk 6:35), who "causes his sun to rise on both the wicked and the good" (Mt 5:45)?

*And keep us from
entering into testing,
but deliver us from
the Evil One
(from evil)*

From the earliest times, the last phrases of the Our Father have been among the most difficult to understand. The problem is not merely a matter of translation. The text of Matthew 6:13 literally reads, "Do not lead us into *peirasmos* (temptation, trial, testing)." The obvious question is to what extent, and why, a God who is our *Abba*, our loving Father, and who wishes to bring us to the fullness of life, would want to make us undergo a temptation or trial.

Christian teachers and pastors have throughout the centuries attempted to explain the phrase in harmony with the Lord's Prayer as a whole and with the rest of the New Testament. Very many things, some good and some not so helpful, have been written and preached on the subject. There are two questions here which can be usefully considered separately—the nuance involved in the verbal construction, and the meaning of the noun *peirasmos*.

First, what can be said about the precise meaning of the verb ("lead us not . . .") in the phrase? Today, a number of scholars are tending toward a simple exegetical explanation. To understand it, we have to learn a bit of grammar.

All the Gospels that have come down to us are written in Greek. The oldest version of the Our Father we possess is therefore written in that language. But we can be virtually certain that Jesus did not say the prayer in Greek but rather in Hebrew or Aramaic. We need not enter into the debate as to which of the two languages Jesus used, since for our purposes they are similar in structure.

The Semitic languages employ a rather small vocabulary or, more exactly, they are able to express a great many notions using relatively few roots, by changing the vowels and by adding prefixes and suffixes. Thus, to express the idea of "leading into," a Semitic would take the verb meaning "to enter" or "to go into" and turn it into a causative, "to make or cause to enter." We can thus conjecture that the original Semitic version of the prayer went something like this: "And do-not-make-enter us into temptation." This sentence can be understood in two different ways. The first is the way the Greek translator understood it, by simply translating the words one after another, "do not make us enter . . .," in other words, "lead us not . . ."

But the phrase could also be understood in another way. It could be rendered "make us not enter . . .," that is to say, "keep us from entering . . ." Gramatically speaking, in fact, this second possibility is more likely, and it has the additional advantage of being in harmony with the rest of Jesus' teaching. Instead of presenting God as someone who takes pleasure in forcing us to undergo a difficult experience, Jesus seems to be telling us to pray for God's help in avoiding . . . something that we are now going to examine.

A rather striking confirmation of this result is given by Jesus' words to the disciples in Gethsemane: "Keep alert and pray so that you do not enter into *peirasmos* (Mt 26:41). This is exactly what we do when we say the Lord's Prayer; we ask God's help in a critical moment during our pilgrimage of faith.

What is this event we need God's assistance to deal with? Unfortunately, no English word exactly captures the biblical nuance of *peirasmos*. The word "temptation" has taken on moralistic, purely negative overtones, whereas the word "trial" is often used as a mere synonym for "difficulty" or "affliction." The word "testing" has the disadvantage of seeming to present God as a strict schoolmaster, but since it is less worn-out than the other alternatives, we will often use it here. It may make us stop and think, which is always beneficial.

To understand the biblical significance of "testing," we need to return once again to the wilderness with the people of Israel. The experience of testing is an integral part of the journey toward the Promised Land, and it always concerns faith, our trust in God.

We have already seen an example of this in the story of the manna (Ex 16). Another classic example is the account of the water from the rock in Exodus 17:1-7. In both cases the Israelites, during their time in the desert, encounter a difficulty, the lack of water or food. This calls into question for them the meaning of their journey. It places a clear alternative before them, with two possible outcomes.

The first possibility is a characteristic reaction of the people. They begin to criticize Moses and thus, indirectly, God. "Did you bring us out of Egypt so we might die?" God is no longer seen as a God of mercy and love, but as the Enemy who desires the destruction of human beings. The technical term for this reaction of the people is the verb "to murmur," "to grumble": the people *grumbled* (Ex 17:3). Another evocative expression is that of "putting God to the test" (Ex 17:2). In order to escape a situation of testing, we may reverse the roles and demand something of God: "If you are really God, you will do this or that for me . . ." This can even lead us in the end to create a god in our own image, instead of following the God who created us in the divine image.

We see the other possible response in the behavior of Moses. He does not know what to do either, but he calls to God: "Lord, help me! Show me the way!" (see Ex 17:4). For Moses, the testing leads to a strengthening of bonds with God, to a greater trust. It is important to realize that, in a situation of testing, we cannot stand still; we must either go forward or backward. An experience of testing leads either to a loss of confidence in God or to a stronger, more mature trust. In the latter case, in an unexpected, paradoxical way, testing helps us go forward on our pilgrimage of faith.

We have also looked at Jesus' trials or temptations in the Gospels (Mt 4:1-11; Lk 4:1-13). Jesus is likewise in the wilderness. But here there is something new: the presence of the Tempter, the "Evil One." The New Testament is more conscious of the presence, in the time of testing, of the powers of evil which attempt to separate us from God and God's love, which try to undermine our trust in God. Sometimes this evil presence is personified, sometimes not, but it is always seen not just as a lack or incompleteness but as a reality threating us especially when we are most vulnerable.

For believers, the important thing is not to become obsessed by the question of evil but simply to understand in what evil consists in order to cope with it. Who has not, in life's difficult moments, heard those voices whispering in their ears, suggesting illusory images of happiness or solutions to problems that take no account of God and our fellow human beings? "God may love other people, but not you . . . If God loves you, why did this happen to you . . .? Think about yourself first; that's the only way to get ahead . . .," and so on. In short, it refers to all those voices, within us or in the world, that try to separate us from trust in God, our *Abba*.

In the Garden of Olives, Jesus encourages his disciples to "keep alert and pray so that you do not enter into temptation" (Mt 26:41). To enter into temptation or testing does not simply mean to be in a difficult situation, for Jesus knows well that the disciples' faith will be put to the test by his arrest and his death. Jesus gives this advice so that his followers will not lose their balance and fall, caught by the wiles of evil like a fly in a spider's web. To enter into testing thus means to fall into the Evil One's trap (see 1 Tm 6:9) by making the Tempter's views our own.

We are now ready to examine what could seem to be a contradiction in the biblical notion of testing. There are some passages that seem to say that God tempts human beings or puts them to the test, whereas other passages categorically deny that God is the author of such an experience. We have seen that testing is part of the journey to the Promised Land; in fact, in the Bible nonbelievers never undergo this experience. So when the Bible seems to say that testing comes from God, this is a shortcut to express that God calls us to follow him, to leave behind our securities and walk with him in the wilderness, when we no longer know what is happening to us and when, in one way or another, our trust in God will be put to the test. God sets us on the road where we will inevitably experience testing.

To go a step further and say, however, that God wishes us to have a difficult time, or even more, that God's desire is for us to "enter into temptation" and stray from the path, would be a horrible blasphemy. God desires precisely the opposite for us—life in all its fullness. God's wish is that, by our trust in him and with his help, we may pass through all the difficulties and finally enter into the fullness of the divine communion.

A passage from the Letter of James shows us both dimensions, one after another, of testing:

Happy the man who withstands testing! Having become tried-and-true, he will receive the crown of life which the Lord has promised to those who love him. Let no one, when they are tested, say that this testing comes from God. For God is incapable of being tested by evil, and he does not test anyone. But each person is tested by their own cravings that lure them on and lead them astray (Jas 1:12-14).

This is not an easy text to translate. Translators often vary the words of *peirasmos/peirazein* to get the meaning across, but then it is not clear that we are dealing with one and the same experience. Here I have used the word "test, testing" each time, even though it makes the English a bit awkward.

Saint James first speaks of the "positive" aspect of testing. Though not good in itself, if one passes through it while continuing to trust in God, testing can lead to a deeper relationship with God. But then the author makes it clear that God is not behind the testing: God does not wish human suffering, and certainly does not want to lead us astray. In this text the source of this negative aspect of the experience of testing which we might call temptation, is located within us—our "divided soul" or "two minds" (Jas 1:8) pulling us in two opposite directions at the same time.

Another text, from Saint Paul, is a good commentary on the last part of the Lord's Prayer:

You have experienced no testing beyond your human capacities. God is trustworthy, and will not let you be tested beyond what you can bear. With the testing, he will also provide a way out and the strength to endure it (1 Cor 10:13).

And so, when we pray "keep us from entering into testing, but deliver us from the Evil One (from evil)," we are not asking to be spared all difficulties in our life. We are calling upon the love of God, convinced that God will give us the strength to pass through the testing and continue on our pilgrimage of faith. We can think once again of the manna in the wilderness: perhaps we would like to accumulate a reserve supply, to be assured, once and for all, that the rest of our life will be easy, but God promises us something else. God assures us of his faithfulness; God tells us that he will always be there beside us during the testing, to show a way out. But more often than not, the way out will not be clear ahead of time.

Those placing their trust in God are not promised an easy life; they are offered God's presence and support. Just before leaving his disciples, Jesus prayed to the Father for them with these words very close to the Our Father: "I do not ask you to take them out of the world, but to protect them from the Evil One" (Jn 17:15). Why are difficulties, times when our faith is put to the test, part of a pilgrimage of trust with God? Why does the road to resurrection go by way of the cross? Who would venture to give an adequate reply to this most agonizing of questions? Yet one thing is clear: whoever agrees to walk with Jesus enters upon the way of love, the way of service. Such people are unwilling to shut their eyes to the problems surrounding them. They refuse to build walls to protect themselves against anything that might harm their private pleasure or comfort. They therefore become more vulnerable to the pain of others. God does not wish us to suffer as an end in itself, But whoever consents to love, consents to suffer.

Moreover, those who attempt to live out gospel values in a world marked by materialism, competition, individualism, and intolerance know that it is not going to be an easy task. Believers often find themselves going against the mainstream and, what is worse, they feel pressures to conform not just from the outside but even within themselves; this can even lead to self-doubt. In our world today, faith is often tested by a kind of inner persecution. This can help us understand Jesus' image of a tiny lamp shining in the darkness, and we can take comfort from his assurance that the shadows will never extinguish the light (Jn 1:5).

In John's Gospel, the final words Jesus speaks to his disciples at the Last Supper sum up well what we having been trying to say:

> I have said these things to you so that in me you may have peace. In the world you are going to have tribulations. But be confident; I have overcome the world (Jn 16:33; see Acts 14:22; Lk 22:28ff.).

Jesus does not promise his disciples an easy life. He even tells them they are going to have trouble. The word translated by "tribulation" has a meaning very close to *peirasmos*, "testing." But Jesus does not stop there. He tells his followers not to lose heart, for he has overcome the world. In other words, the love of God become tangible in the death and resurrection of God's Son reveals itself to be stronger than all the powers of evil. And this assurance is, for those who take it to heart, a source of *peace*, that inner peace which comes from God and which enables us to continue our journey amidst all the difficulties which may occur. Rooted in this peace, we become able to bring peace to others.

And so at the end of the Lord's Prayer, we remind ourselves that the road of discipleship does not meaning taking the easy way out. We entrust ourselves to God's assistance, in the assurance that this will enable us to pass through all the difficulties which may arise. And we express our confidence that this assistance will always be given when the time for it comes. By this petition we reject all false self-confidence in order to place our confidence, once again, in our *Abba* who takes care of us.

## Questions for Reflection

1. When our faith is tested, we sometimes try to find a way out in a nostalgic and illusory vision of the past (see Nm 11:5-6). Or we may create a caricature of God in order to rebel against it (see Nm 20:4-5; Jer 15:18). What forms could such practices take in our own life? What can we do to escape from them?

2. How does the paschal mystery, Christ's journey through suffering and death to the fullness of life, provide a key for understanding our own existence as we try to follow him (see Mk 8:34-37; Jn 12:24-26; Rom 6:3-11; Phil 3:10-12; 1 Pt 2:21-25)?

# "Here I am; send me"

(Is 6:8)

Let us now attempt, at the end of our reflections, to grasp the impressive unity of this great prayer of Jesus, the Our Father.

By its first words, the most essential ones, we express that Jesus, by his gift of the Holy Spirit, brings us into a new relationship with God, which leads immediately to a new relationship among human beings. It is as if when we say "Our Father in heaven," we let Jesus take us by the hand and lead us into the Father's house (see Jn 14:2). To put it in more theological terms, we enter into the communion of the Holy Trinity. We share the common life of God, and in this way are transformed into God's image to a greater and greater degree.

While still making our home in the Father's house, we have to set out on a journey. Living in God's house can never be a privilege for a chosen few. Jesus invites us to take part in a *pilgrimage* with him, to widen this communion to include the whole of creation. This is the significance of the three petitions that form the first part of the Lord's Prayer: hallowed be your name, your Kingdom come, your will be done ... We are praying that the entire world may discover

God's true identity and live in consequence, and we give our life to God so that, through us, God can share this divine life with others. So we set out on pilgrimage in order to witness to God's love and light even in the simplest realities of our existence.

Jesus tells us not to take any provisions with us for the journey (see Lk 9:3). This is a pilgrimage of *trust*: at each stage God will give us all we need. God offers us three gifts, named in the second part of the Lord's Prayer. First, God offers us material and spiritual support, bread which is, in the final analysis, Christ himself. Second, God offers us forgiveness so that we can always begin our journey again. Even if yesterday we were inattentive to the call, God remains faithful; by forgiveness God sets us back on the road today. And finally, God offers us assistance especially at times when we are most vulnerable, so that our trials themselves can be transformed into springboards which can allow us to go even further ahead; the valley of tears can become a place of living springs (see Ps 84:6). In this way our pilgrimage resembles more and more closely that of Jesus, his paschal mystery which transfigured death into a road to endless life.

The prayer that Jesus taught us thus expresses, in great simplicity, the very heart of our faith. We will never finish finding gospel treasures in it. It is a prayer able to nourish, our whole life long, a pilgrimage of trust on earth.

## Questions for Reflection

1. Read the last prayer of Jesus in John 17. What themes of the Our Father can you discover in it?

2. The following questions can help make the Our Father relevant to us today: Who is the God I encounter through Jesus Christ? How can I, in the footsteps of Christ, transmit to others by the life I lead something of this living God? What gifts does God offer me to accomplish this calling? How can I make these gifts my own?